ETSY

Launch Your Handmade Empire!—Blueprint to Opening a Storefront on Etsy and Growing Your Business

By: Marianna Hart

Free Bonus: Join Our Book Club and Receive Free Gifts Instantly

Click Below For Your Bonus: https://success321.leadpages.co/freebodymindsoul/

TABLE OF CONTENTS

INTRODUCTION

When it comes to selling your own homemade products, the market can be tough. Perhaps you have tried going on a few online sites or concentrate your efforts to working at flea markets and farmer's markets n the hopes of making a few sales. People like your products, but you just aren't making the amount of money that you like. If this sounds like your own homemade business, it may be time to consider going with Etsy.

Etsy is one of the best online markets that you can find for artists with homemade items. People all over the world are looking for products that are unique or ones that they just can not readily get in their own area. As the artist, you will be able to set up your own shop right on the site and have the ability to reach thousands of people, or more, all over the world. Your business can start to grow and you can finally earn what you have always wanted with your own work.

This guidebook is going to show you the steps that you need to take in order to get started with Etsy and actually make your business grow like crazy. Unfortunately, it is not enough to create a few products, take some pictures, and post them to bring in the customers. There are thousands of other sellers who are doing the exact same thing each day. But this guidebook will help you to understand the steps that you need to do to make your shop stand out.

In this guidebook we will discuss many of the different aspects of Etsy selling and how to market your products. We will start out by talking over what Etsy is and some of the best products that you can try to sell if you are still uncertain about what you would like to work in. Then we will move on to the basics of setting up your own shop. For those who are already to this point, check out chapter 4 because we provide a great marketing plan, along with some good tips, that will help you to get your shop at the top of lists and really bring in the sales.

The final chapter in this book will spend some time talking about some of the do's and do nots of getting started with Etsy. This is a great chapter to visit if you are a beginner to Etsy because there are many helpful hints that can put your shop at the top of the list.

Your Etsy shop has the potential to make you a lot of money and really can grow your business more than ever before. But you need to use some of the tips in this book and grow your own marketing strategy as much as you can in order to entice the customers and get them to come to you for their next handmade product.

CHAPTER ONE
GETTING STARTED WITH ETSY

The internet has brought us so many great updates to make life better. You can shop for your groceries, presents, and other things online. You can run your own business from the comfort of your own home. You can talk to people on the other side of the world just like they were next to you. There is just so much that you can do with being online.

One movement that has really been moving in this world is the work from home business. You can sell health and medical products, as well as jewelry, candy, and makeup, to people you know and meet along the way. You can become a freelance writer, work in computers, make classes and programs for people to follow, take surveys and so much more.

Many people are starting their own businesses by creating a product and selling it online. Homemade products are really popular; customers want to have these homemade products even though they do not know how to make them, or do not have the time, and they will pay to have someone do it for them. This is a huge opportunity to make a good income on the side or full time as long as you can do fantastic work or create something that is completely new.

If you do decide to sell some of your own homemade products online, there are several choices that you can make when picking a site to sell them on. But one of the most popular sites that you should check out is Etsy. This guidebook will spend some time looking at Etsy and how you can get started with your very own homemade business using it!

What is Etsy?

Etsy is an online marketplace where people all over the world are able to connect in order to make, buy, and sell unique goods. The global community can help to bring about some of the most unique items that you won't be able to find anywhere else, bringing together different cultures, areas, and ideas when it comes to the products produced.

If you are someone who likes to make homemade crafts or you have some great products that are unique and unusual, you will want to check out Etsy. This is the first place that a lot of sellers will head to if they want a one of a kind gift that they are not able to find anywhere else. You can fill this need as long as you are able to make great products, that are original (no copying from anywhere else), and that the customer will enjoy.

The biggest benefit of using Etsy is that you will be able to find products that you would not be able to find anywhere else. These are mostly homemade products made by small businesses and these manufacturers will choose to go with Etsy to advertise and sell their products.

Some of the things that things that sellers will enjoy about Etsy include:

- The ability to discover vintage goods, handmade items, and craft supplies. Often it is hard to find these items anywhere else.

- Get recommendations that are based on your personal tastes.

- Find flea markets, crat fairs, and boutiques where you can shop from these sellers offline if you would like to see the products first hand.

There are also a like of great reasons to choose Etsy when you are a seller. These include:

- You can open up an Etsy shop for just $0.20 and you can post anything that you would like to sell. Handmade items are the most popular, but your imagination is the limit.

- Grow your own business, on your own terms. Etsy makes it easy.

- Reach your customers no matter where they are. You aren't limited to just your geographical area.

Etsy is a great shop to work with for both buyers and sellers. First, sellers are gong to enjoy all the unique options that are available. If you are looking for something in particular and can not find it around you or you want a unique item for a gift, Etsy is often the best place to start because of all the options. Be careful though; after looking around for just a bit of time, you will find that there are so many great items to choose from and your shopping cart may get pretty full.

Using Etsy as a seller is a great option as well. It is easy to set up an account and you can add a lot of great products to your store without all the hassle. Your market is going to be huge as well; rather than being stuck with your small demographics, you can choose to reach the whole world, making your target market much bigger. Add in the ability to change things around and even to design coupons, and this site is really easy for sellers to use.

No matter what product you are working with, you will find that working with Etsy can be a great experience. Unlike some of the other product selling sites that are looking for the product to be sold at the store or have a specific number to be successful, Etsy allows you to be completely unique and bring your own story to the products that you sell.

Take a look around Etsy, you are going to find a lot of products that you would never find anywhere else, besides maybe at a few craft fairs in your area. If you start to look at some of the products that are sold overseas, you may find that you can only get these items on Etsy.

This is because Etsy is completely unique and original. It values crafters, home workers, and those that are able to create a completely original product. You will find that the buyers who come to these sites are looking to get a good product, one that they aren't able to find anywhere else, for that special someone or for themselves. If they wanted a regular every day product, they would go to Walmart or Amazon to make their purchase.

This makes it the perfect opportunity for you. If you are able to work on a craft that is completely new and unique, you are going to be able to make some money with Etsy. If you are in to crafting, making something that is new, and having fun from your home, whether you are doing this full time or not, you have a place when you are on Etsy.

If you are stuck for ideas on what you should do when you are selling on Etsy, just remember that anything can work. Take a look through the Etsy site and see which products are the most popular and which ones you may be able to make something similar. Of course, do not work on making the same item because this is not going to do you any favors with the buyers, but it is a good idea to find out what is popular and what you may want to do.

Do you have a lot of ideas and want to do some work in different categories to mix things up and to make it easier to get a lot more sales? This is something that you can do as well. We will discuss this a bit more in later chapters, but you will be able to make more than one "shop" within Etsy so that you can sell different products in different categories without making too much of a mess in your shop.

There is just so much that you are able to do when you work on Etsy. It is a completely unique site that brings together artisans from different backgrounds and crafting abilities and helps them to sell to buyers who are the most interested in something that is completely unique and one of a kind.

The Benefits of Etsy

As a seller, there are a lot of different websites that you may be able to choose to sell your products. But you want to choose the one that is the easiest to use and will reach the biggest market. Etsy is often the first choice that sellers and buyers alike will check out because it is easy to use and has so many great products available. Some of the benefits for a seller to choose Etsy over some of the other sites that you could choose from include:

- A community available—the Etsy community is amazing for new and professional individuals who want to make and sell their crafts. You can ask questions, learn from others, and just make some great networking bonds.

- Custom orders—it is really easy for you to customize orders on Etsy for your customers.

- Less competition—with other sites, you are not only competing with craft items, but also with items that have nothing to do with crafting. This can make it harder to make any income from them. With Etsy, you will only have to compete with craft items.

- Easy to list special items—you can have specialty items, one of a kind items, and other choices on your Etsy account.

- Work with others—if you choose, you can set up a store that has other crafters working along with you.

- Buyers setting the stage—there are times when a buyer can approach you and personally ask for commissioned work. This helps you to take on other orders that you may not have thought about before but which you can easily do.

- The site is popular—this is the biggest site to visit for both artists and customers so you will be able to find the customers that you want for your products.

Of course, there are some benefits that come for the buyers who visit the site, which is why so many of them keep coming back to get more items. They like the idea that there are a wide variety of sellers and items that they can check out. They may like a homemade item but just aren't able to make that item on their own. In some cases they want to find something that is completely one of a kind and unique, for themselves, for a friend, or even for a special occasion, and so they will choose to go onto Etsy to find what they need.

When you are able to meet these needs, you are going to make some great sales. With the help of the marketing ideas in this guidebook, a good looking shop, and some great products, you are going to be able to fill this need with the customer and get them to come back to your shop again and again.

Working with Etsy is one of the best decisions that you can make for your business. Even if you have your own website that you use, it is always a good idea to go with an Etsy account too. This helps you to increase your views, find more customers, and can make things easier than taking care of your own website. With all of the great benefits that come from using Etsy, it is no wonder that so many artists and sellers choose to go with this option.

Are there other sites like Etsy?

One question that a lot of people will have is whether there are other sites that are like Etsy. Yes, there are some other sites like Etsy, but none of them are going to give you the same reach and the same customer base as you will find with Etsy. You may want to consider some of these other options in order to really expand your business to reach as many customers as possible, but the best place to go is with Etsy.

Most of the other crafting sites are going to be kind of small and not as interactive and easy to use as Etsy. You may have tried a few of them in the past and not found success. Have you ever tried to sell your products on Amazon or eBay? These are world renowned sites and you have probably purchased a few items from these sites, but they focus more on movies, books, electronics and more rather than focusing on the hand crafted and homemade products. You can try to sell your products on these sites, but you just won't see the results that you want from this business endeavor.

Some people choose to go with online craft shops, such as on Facebook, but this is not that effective either. Most of these are going to be for local areas so your market is a whole lot smaller than you would find with Etsy and you are competing against other people you know for the same customers. When it comes to some that are for a whole state or larger, there are usually so many people on these sites and no way to use SEO or other options, that it is not really going to help you at all to give them a try.

Basically, while there are some other options that you are able to go with for selling your crafts and other products, none of them are going to compare to what you can get with Etsy. It does a lot of the work for you, helping you to get the shop set up, sell a wide variety of products, and so much more. If you are ready to start earning some real income from your talents and maybe even making this into a full time gig, it is never a bad idea to go with Etsy!

CHAPTER TWO
THE BEST PRODUCTS TO SELL ON ETSY

As we explored in the previous chapter, Etsy is a great place to sell lots of homemade and unique items. People want to purchase something that is unique and will set them apart, perhaps as something nice to have in their home or to give as a gift. If you already specialize in making something in particular, you should stick with that and set up your shop to sell on Etsy.

Pretty much anything that you would like to sell is going to work great on Etsy. As long as you find something that is unique and it is homemade, you will find that you will get some purchases with the right marketing campaign. People are always looking for some great gift items that will help them stand out or make it look like they worked hard on the product and they will head to Etsy in order to find the best option for them.

But if you are simply looking for some ideas on how to get started, you may be unsure of what you should sell on this site. There are many choices in homemade products, but which ones are the easiest to work on, the ones that won't take up more time and money than you would make from the process, and will help you to make a good profit. Here is a list of some of the best products that you can consider selling on Etsy.

Supplies

First we will look at supplies. This is one of the biggest sellers on Etsy and can include pretty much anything that people would use to make a craft such as beads, wax, buttons, thread, and various materials. The benefit of selling these supplies on Etsy is that for the most part, your customers are already on Etsy. Other crafters and sellers of Etsy will look around to find the supplies that they need to complete their own projects and products. If you have these available for a decent price, you could get some repeat sales from others in the same industry since shopping on Etsy is easy and convenient for them.

There are many different kinds of supplies that you can choose to sell on Etsy. You will sometimes find the average supplies that are found at a craft store. These are still popular since it is more convenient to order online, especially for those who may live some distance from a craft store. There are also many unique supplies that you can find such as custom made beads and dyed fabric. There really is no limit to what a seller can provide in the supplies industry.

Supplies can be a fun category to get into. You will need to have some access to really good deals on these products or some that are unusual and unique. Remember that the majority of your clients are going to be other sellers and they need to be able to keep their costs low in this process so that they can make a profit off selling to their customers. If you are able to get your products at a really good discount and then sell them to others, you can make a good profit.

On the other hand, you may need to go with a product that is unique. This can increase the product price a bit more plus can make it easier to find a seller who would pay a bit higher price. Unique items are popular on Etsy when it comes to supplies because it helps the other sellers are going to want these kinds of products to set their own apart.

Bath and beauty

Another great industry to get into on Etsy is bath and beauty products. These would include things like makeup, lotions, soaps, shampoos, perfumes, and other such products. Studies have shown that many teens and women will shop on Etsy to find these products. If you are able to provide these items in a wide variety of shapes, packaging, colors, and scents, your market increases even more.

There are two benefits to using this category. First, women and teens are likely to purchase these products for themselves. They may like the idea of purchasing homemade products or want to avoid the harmful chemicals that come from many store brands. Another market that you can get is during the holidays; it is common for many individuals to purchase these kinds of products for coworkers, loved ones, and others they need to purchase a gift for during the year.

There are a few different things that you can do in order to keep up with selling in this category. Some people will choose to just sell one kind of item, such as going with bath bombs or lotions. This is a great way to get really good at your product and make sure that you can provide many unique and new options within that category.

For the most part, people will sell a variety of these. They may have some lotions, some soaps, shampoos, bath bombs, and so on to make the shop fill out and to hopefully make a few different sales. This is a great way to increase your reach on Etsy and to make it easier for the client to be able to find you.

One thing to consider when you are working in the bath and beauty industry of Etsy is to make gift sets. A lot of people are going to go onto Etsy to look for a variety of gifts, including holiday, birthday, wedding, and more gifts. When you can package together a few of your products and make it into an attractive presentation, you are going to be able to make a lot more sales from people who are looking for a simple gift for someone or those who waited until the last minute to purchase that gift.

The downside to using these products is allergies. Make sure that you are listing the various products you put in the products just in case someone is allergic. Be available to answer questions in case someone is curious about whether your product will be safe for them to use or not.

Girls' Clothing

Clothing of all kinds sell well on Etsy so if you have a knack for creating outfits or can add something special to the different outfits, you can really get something out of it. But it seems that toe category of girls' clothing is really popular on Etsy. And having a full wardrobe of options available on your site can make a big difference so make sure to have shoes, onesies, dresses, hats, and other items for the customer to choose from.

If you happen to already be selling some clothing on your site, consider adding in some little girls' clothes as well. This will help to get more customers to your site and you would be surprised at how big of a seller these items can be on your shop page.

There are a lot of cute clothing items that you are able to choose when you are working on Etsy. You will be able to add in pants, shorts, skirts, dresses, tutu dresses, and so much more. Add in some sparkles, some frills, and some funny sayings, and you are going to be able to get a lot of mothers and relatives who would like to make a purchase.

Next on the list is baby items. People are always interested in cute little outfits and accessories for babies, especially if they are on the way to a baby shower and aren't sure what else to cut. If you have a wide selection of some of these items in your shop, you will be able to entice a few buyers in to make a sale.

Clothing in general does well on Etsy so if you have a wide variety of clothing available, you can do a great job. Perhaps highlight some of the girls and baby clothing and then make sure that they link up to some of the other clothing options for the buyer to take a look at. Or you can have some matching outfits, such as mother daughter outfits, so that your customers have some options that will make them spend more at your shop. This may make it easier for you to earn a few sales all in once.

Jewelry

Another area where you can sell well is jewelry. Of course, you need to make sure that the jewelry you are selling is handmade and unique. These items are often popular because they are different from the rest or they can be customized to fit a certain need. Many of your clients will be interested in finding jewelry like this for Christmas gifts, anniversaries, and birthdays.

There are many different types of jewelry that you can consider making, such as anklets, bracelets, earrings, necklaces, and rings, and including a wide variety of these in your shop will increase the chances that a customer will pick your shop. Mix and match some sets, try out something new, and have lots of variety in order to offer the right option to your clients. Some sellers offer customization too so that a customer is able to make some changes and suggestions if they can not find something for their needs.

One of the best ways that you can sell jewelry is to make some of your own. This is going to ensure that you are making jewelry that is completely original and unique. If you go with this method though, make sure that you are picking high quality materials that will make the jewelry stand out. No one wants to spend a lot of money on a necklace or other piece of jewelry just to have it break a few weeks down the line. The higher quality will help you to get better reviews and will ensure that you are going to get more repeat sales.

Another option is to choose is to purchase jewelry that you found somewhere else. There are a lot of wholesale sites that you can go to that will sell nice jewelry for a good price and you will be able to make a profit from some of these. Or you can choose to go to garage sales or other locations to find some nice options that your customers will like.

It doesn't really matter where you are getting the jewelry, just make sure that you are picking out pieces that are unique, once that look nice, and ones that are going to have high quality materials so that the customer will be happy with their purchase.

Things to consider

When selling on Etsy, remember that there are hundreds of other sellers trying to make a profit as well. You need to make the item unique in order to get the views and the sales. If you are just choosing one of these categories because it is on the top of the list, you may not be as successful as you wish. But if you are able to take one of these categories and make it completely unique, you will find that the customers are ready to check out your shop and make a purchase. You just need to find the niche that is right for you and then really work your business to be unique online.

The best thing for you to sell is something that you love to make. If you already enjoy making something that is on this list, then go ahead and make some of these. But if your passion is in something else, then you should go for that. Your customers are going to notice the difference between products that are made just to make money and those that are made with a lot of love and attention. Even if your favorite items to make aren't on this list, set up a shop and get to selling because you will be amazed at how many people will be willing to make a purchase on these unique items.

Getting started on Etsy can seem intimidating in the beginning. But one of the first things that you should decide on is what you would like to sell to the customers. Even if your particular craft for sale is not on the list above, you can still bring in the customers as long as your item is unique and unlike anything else that is found on the site. Find the niche that is right for you and make it shine and the customers will come.

CHAPTER THREE
SETTING UP YOUR WORKSPACE

While quite a bit of your business is going to take place online, you will still need to make sure that you have enough space to work on the products. Where are you going to create the projects? Where are you going to keep your supplies? Where are you going to take the pictures that you post up? These are important questions to ask.

You need to have some form of organization going on in your business. And that includes with your own workspace. You need to set aside some place inside of your home, or even a little office, where you are able to keep everything in order, find the things that you need, and where all of your items for the business can stay together.

Too many beginners do not have a plan for how they will complete their work. They will spend a lot of time working on their marketing plan and making the shop look nice, and hopefully getting a few customers. But how are they going to operate once they get a few orders. You may be able to work within your living room on the first few orders, but if you are running this as a business, you will be aiming to get lots of orders, and stuffing the information in a corner or all over the place is just going to become a disaster.

You need to treat our Etsy business just like a regular business and have some organization. Before starting, find a room, or at least a corner, of your home and make that just for the business. Leave all of your supplies, your computer, your receipts, and anything else that you will need to run the business in that area. Do not allow anyone else to be there and make sure that you aren't adding other things to the area.

This will help you to be able to find things all in one place. When you are ready to get to work, you can sit down and get started without worrying about losing information, trying to find what you need, or just getting frustrated. You can keep the supplies organized so you know when you are running out of things, have your completed orders in one folder, and so much more. Organization is key to getting your business off the ground and to get the best results possible with your Etsy store.

Picking a place to work

The place you pick to do your work is really important. You need to have a place that is out of the way, a place that won't get in the way of other family members going about their day so that no one else messes around with anything there. You may want to choose your own room, a basement, or just a corner that is out of the way.

If you are able to, pick a place that is quiet. This allows you to get to work without having a lot of distractions along the way. You will be able to concentrate on the work, take orders, answer questions, and do everything without having a whole bunch of people running around and making it hard to keep up with the work that you need to get to.

Any place in your home can work, as long as you are able to get the work done. Make sure that it is big enough that you are able to put all of your supplies but, otherwise it is possible to work in any location of your home.

Supplies for your Etsy store

You will also need to have a few supplies on hand to get your business up and running. While each store is going to need some different supplies based on the product that they are trying to sell, there are a few things that you can have on hand no matter what kind of product you are selling. Some of the supplies that you will need include:

- Computer—you need to have a decent computer ready to work with. You are going to spend some time on your computer, working on your Etsy store, working on social media, and checking to see if there are any new orders to complete while also answer some questions along the way. You need a computer that is pretty quick, one that is going to make it easy to keep up with all of your new tasks and won't die on you all of the time. If you do not already have a good laptop or desktop computer, you need to consider investing in one. This is one of the things that you can deduct on your taxes later on as long as you use this computer primarily for your new Etsy shop business.

- Printer—there are going to be times when you will need to use a printer. If you want to print of receipts to send to the customer, shipping labels, or some other information. Invest in a high quality printer that will be able to keep up with the workload that you are hoping to get.

- Desk space—a desk, a table, or some other place where you can work on your products for sale can be nice. The item that you use will sometimes vary depending on what you work with, but make it your own. Make sure that there is enough room to organize your information and to keep all your materials in place.

- Good tax software—do not forget that you will need to do taxes at the end of the year on any of the money that you make. Any time that you make more than $600 during the year, including the money that you make with your regular job and your Etsy store, you are going to have to report it. Consider getting a good tax software that will help you to keep track of your expenses as well as your profits so that you can get your taxes done without a lot of hassle.

- Packing boxes and supplies—you need to have a few things on hand that will help you to ship off the products that you are selling. You can choose to go to the post office each time you have an order, but this is not an efficient way to run your business. It is better to purchase some of the supplies ahead of time and have them around the house so you can send off multiple orders at once. You should also have some tape, packing supplies to go in the box, and even more to make the shipping process as easy as possible.

Setting up your work space is important. It helps you to have an area where all of your materials and supplies are in one place without losing anything or wasting your time. Make sure to find an area where only your work things are going to belong and keep everything organized there to prevent procrastination or lost materials along the way.

CHAPTER FOUR

HOW TO SET UP YOUR ETSY SHOP

Now that we know a little bit more about Etsy and have had the time to pick out which product we would like to sell, it is time to get to work setting up your Etsy shop. The Etsy shop is the part that customers will see when they are looking at your product. On your end, it is the area where you will list all of your items and keep track of sales, products, and other information you need.

For the customer, they will be able to click on one product they maybe like, but also have other items show up from your store. If they like these, they can click on them and get taken to the store and see all the great options that you have available. It is like shopping in a real store but online once your customer gets to this point. Whether they go all the way in to your store to look at all the options or just check out the first page on an item they like, the customer will be able to make a purchase from you.

As you can see, the Etsy shop is an important aspect of your marketing plan and you need to take some time to get it all set up. Here we will look at some of the steps that you should take in order to make your Etsy shop look amazing in no time so that you can bring in those sales.

Opening up the shop

When you are ready to open up the shop, go onto the Etsy page and click on the top left hand of the screen where the sell button is. Etsy is really great for walking you through all the steps that are needed to open the shop and make your first listing appear. You should be able to get it set up pretty quickly and can start selling before long.

It is a good idea to set up a name that you really like. While Etsy does allow you to make changes to the name if you would like to in the future, setting up a name that you will stick with can make things easier. Your customers will have trouble finding you and your products if you always change the name and it is so much easier to start branding yourself if the name stays the same. Consider carefully what you would like your store to be named and stick with that.

Another thing to note is that you will need to keep a credit card on file with your account. This is the way that Etsy will bill you for the fees that come with your listing. You can choose to go with PayPal if you would like, but Etsy is going to ask you to keep the credit card on file anyway.

Some beginners may be excited to sell a multitude of products on their shop. You are allowed to sell as many products as you would like on Etsy, but you do need to be careful about making your shop too full and crowded. If you are selling several different categories of products, such as supplies and clothes, consider using this step twice to make a few different stores. This may seem like a lot of extra effort, but it is gong to help you to keep things organized, prevents your store from looking too crowded, and will make it easier to sell the items that you want.

Customizing the shop

Now that you have your shop signed up, it is time to get the shop looking great. You want to spend some time customizing the site so that it looks amazing and has some of your personal touch. Think of this kind of like your real personal store at a mall or another location. It would have certain designing and placement so that it had the feel and look that would stick with your customers.

This is the same with your online store. You want to make sure that your personality will show through. Your store and your products are going to become your brand and you should make this show through in the store. This section will take some time to look at how you can customize your shop to make it really stand out.

1. Profile picture—you can add an avatar or a picture for your seller profile. You can pick out a profile picture that you like and anything will do, but since you are trying to make money from this, you should pick out something that looks professional. You can do a nice picture of yourself, add your logo, or add in something else that works well with your business. You can always change the profile picture later if you feel the need.

2. Header—another part of the shop that you are able to personalize is the header. You need to pick something that is 760 X 100 pixels. Pick something that will really make your business stand out and can show the customers that you are a real business. Of course, you can always change it if you want to. Etsy does have some premade headers if you would like to use these to get started, or you can make some yourself.

3. Shop title—the title of your shop is kind of like the tagline. If you have a shop name that doesn't fully say what you sell, your shop title should be able to help out with this. It is going to show up in Google searches, as well as in the storefront for your shop. This makes it really important if you want to catch some customers through

SEO or online searches. Give your shop title a bit of thought to get the best results.

4. Domain name and email—you can consider having a domain name as well as an email that go along with your shop. This can help you to start your own personal website or a blog that will promote the shop. Make sure that they are available on Etsy before making the purchase so you do not waste your time. Check out Bluehost and Namecheap to make the right decision on a domain name.

5. Banners—there is also the option to add in some banners to the Etsy shop. This will make it easier to set yourself apart and can really help to set the theme for your shop. Take the time to make this part look amazing so that your shop will stick with your customers long after they are done visiting.

While you are working on the main part of the site, you need to make sure that you are working on your terms and policies in the process. This can be really helpful to the customers and will protect you in case something goes wrong. You can put your requirements for shipping and returns, whether you will allow customization and what kinds, and other information that will save trouble later on and helps the customer make an informed decision.

Picking the best products to show

If you are just starting out, you may only have a few products that you are able to sell. This is perfectly fine, as long as you make them really high quality and can showcase them with great pictures on the website. On the other hand, if you have quite a few products that you are ready to sell, it is time to pick some of the best ones. As a beginner, you do not want to post hundreds of products to your page right away. This is an option, but you are missing out on some of the great benefits to posting the new items slowly.

If you post everything at once, your customer only gets one chance to see your work. But if you post maybe ten to twenty items and then slowly add on two more each week or so, you are allowing your shop to be on the first page again and again each week. Etsy will offer the benefit of new products being featured on the front page. You will not be on the front page for long, but even a few minutes is better than nothing. Spreading out the postings can allow you to announce new products, even if they're older, and makes it easier for new customers to see you.

So if you are faced with the dilemma of which products to post, consider which ones look the best, which ones are the most unique, and which ones you enjoy making the most. Pick a few and then take amazing pictures before uploading to your site.

You will be able to post those and make a few sales and then regularly update some of the other products later. None of your products are going to be left out, you are just using a smarter way to post so that you get more customers with less work.

Posting your first product

Once you have had the time to mess around with your Etsy shop and get it to look the way that you want, it is time to post your first product. This is pretty easy to do, but make sure that you are gong about it right so that the product shows up when someone is searching for it.

The first thing you should do is come up with a name for the product. Think about what words people would use when searching for your product and try to include those in the title as well.

Next, you need to write out a short description of the product. This doesn't have to be real in depth, but it will help to explain a bit more about the product to help the customer out. This is another place to put in some more keywords so that your products are more likely to show up on Etsy as well as on a Google search from the customer. Take some time to write out the descriptions or if you are not that great with writing out the words, consider hiring a professional to do some of the work.

Now it is time to take some pictures. Your customers will never make a purchase if they have no idea what your product looks like. Take at least a few high quality pictures of your item to post along with the product so that the customer can see if this is similar to what they are looking for.

Some people feel that they need to post a different listing for each variance in the product they are selling. For example, if they are selling a scarf, they may feel that they need to have a posting for every color or combination of color they are willing to provide to the customer. While you can do this, it will take a lot of time and can really clog up your shop if you are selling other products. A better option is to just have one posting, with a few pictures of the different options, and then explain to the customer the different options that they are able to purchase. Then all the information comes in to one place and you can make the changes when working.

Your first product posting is one of the most important. This is going to be one of the first things that your customers are going to see when they come to your page and you want it to look good. Sure, you are probably going to send out at least a few products at a time so that your shop doesn't look empty, but make sure that these are some of your best products and that the pictures and the set up look amazing to impress your customers.

Remember the price

And then you should remember to put the price on your product. If you are unsure about how much to charge, take a look at some of the similar products that are available on Etsy. This will give you a good starting point to put up there. Remember that sometimes you can go a bit higher if you feel that your product is superior in some way to the other options, but do not go crazy here or you won't get any sales.

You need to remember that you are not only selling the price of the materials that you purchased to make the product, but you also need to price out the shipping expenses, the time and energy that you put into the product, and how much you would like to make. Too many beginners try to pick the lowest price in the hopes of getting more customers. You may get some customers out of doing this, but if you end up losing money in the process, you are not going to end up ahead.

Even if you need to price a bit higher than some of the competitors, it doesn't mean that you won't get some of the customers that you want. Customers realize when things are high quality and they know how much these products are worth. While some of them will go for the cheaper item because they are on a budget or do not have much to spend, there are still plenty of other customers who want something that is high quality and unique. If you can provide this to the customer, even if it costs a bit more, you will still get some customers with the right marketing.

 Once all of this information is ready and in place on the Etsy site, you are ready to start selling your product. You will be able to hit the submit button and all that information is going to show up on your store. This is one of the first steps to starting your shop and while you will still need to do some marketing and other work, it is a great place to get started.

Once the product is ready, you can make it live for customers to see. Now it will be available on Etsy. Unfortunately, you will need to do some more work, perhaps add in some more products as well, before you see the big sales, but we will discuss more of the marketing strategy in the next chapter.

CHAPTER FIVE

DOING SOME MARKET RESEARCH ON ETSY

Another thing that you should spend some time on when working on Etsy is market research. This is going to really help your products to do better and can help you with everything from picking out the right site to work on, picking out your keywords, and even choosing which other products to design if you want to add to your store.

When you get into selling on Etsy, your main goal is to make a profit. Market research is going to help give you a good picture of what is going on in the market and to tell you how well your products are going to do. you will be able to research the different questions that you have and can often help you to figure out the next steps that you want to take.

Types of research

There are two main types of research that you can do with your market research, primary and secondary research. Both of thee going to help you to gather and analyze data to determine how you can run your shop. You will need to talk to some potential customers, even if they are just some people that you already know, and take a look at some of your competitors' shops to see how you can manage yours for better results.

Both types of research are important to your marketing plan. They are going to help you to get the valuable information that you need to really set your shop apart from some of the other Etsy shops that you are competing with. While primary research is going to help you to get the information directly from customers, secondary research has its place as well, helping you to learn more about your competitors and to get a foot up on the market. Some of the things that you should know about primary research and secondary research for your marketing plan include:

Primary research

The first research that you should start out with is primary research. The goal with primary research is to gather your data from current practices and sales of those who are being successful. It is going to take the plans of your competitors' into account and can even give you some valuable information about your competitors. Some of the ways that you can collect this primary research includes:

- Interviews

- Surveys

- Questionnaires

- Focus groups

You do not have to go all out and spend hours on these things, but perhaps go onto your Facebook account and ask a few people if they would not mind taking a short survey to help you out. Keep the questions short and simple and even offer an incentive for them to check you out. It can provide you with some valuable insights, perhaps helping you to learn which products will sell best and which ones aren't worth your time.

Secondary research

The goal of using secondary research is to look at data that has already been published. This would be like going out and looking up information in a book or magazine. You are able to get some valuable information that saves time, but you are not getting the direct information yourself. This is a good way to identify the target segments you want to work with, identify your competitors and so much more. This is one of the best ways to figure out your targeted demographic and how you will market to them.

Secondary research can be a great way to get some of the information that you need about the customer. If you do not have a lot of people who you can talk to directly or you would like to learn more about your competition and how they are doing things, then using secondary research can really help you to get the information that you need.

Collect the data

Your business is not going to succeed if you can not learn how to understand your customers, the services that you are offering and how they will benefit the customer, and the whole market in general. There is a lot of competition in Etsy and you may find hundreds, if not more, sellers who are going to be offering the same products as you. If you aren't doing market research, you are allowing your competition to get the best of you and missing out on critical information that you need.

Here are two types of data collection that you can choose from, and in all reality you should be using both. Quantitative is the first one and it is going to require a really large sample size. The results of this data is going to give you a lot of information really quickly. You may send out a large survey to your 500 friends on Facebook and ask for answers from all of them, even if some may never purchase from your store.

This one can be good because it gives you a general idea of how the market is working, even if everyone is not going to choose to purchase from you. You can get a good look into the mind of the whole market and maybe develop some plans that will allow you to sell to these people later on.

On the other hand, qualitative research is going to spend more time on the quality rather than the quantity of the information that you have. You may only ask 10 people to answer your questions, but these are people who fit your target audience and who may actually purchase one of your products in the future. This is like talking directly to the customer and it can give you a lot of valuable information in the process.

Make sure to get a wide variety of research. This will ensure that you are getting the most accurate information for setting up your store and getting the right products out there to your customers.

Common mistakes in your marketing

Many beginners are strapped for money and for time and assume that they can take some shortcuts when it comes to making their marketing plan. Some of the shortcuts that you should avoid because they will backfire on you as a beginner include:

- Only going with the secondary research—yes, this is the easiest to get ahold of because you do not have to do as much work, but it is not as efficient as the primary research. The primary research lets you learn about what is going on now in the industry, not what happened a year or more ago. You can ask specific questions, find people who are actually in your target audience, and more. It is always best to get at least a little bit of primary research to help you make the best decisions.

- Using only resources that you find from the web—when you choose to go on common search engines, you may be able to find out a lot of information, but this is the same information that is available to everyone else. You could mix out on some important information that is just for your business. You should also go to other sources, doing interviews, looking at your local library, college campuses, and other locations to perform your research and find the answers that you need.

- Interviewing only those that you know—this is a good place to start since some of them may be willing to purchase from you, but this is not where the surveying should start. You need to get out there and talk to people who are actually your customers, people who do not know you but may actually purchase your products. Go and visit local shops, find others on social media, and look around to find out who may be willing to make a purchase of your product so that you can get some of the valuable information that is needed to run your business.

Setting up a good marketing plan is critical to your success on Etsy. It is going to help you to determine the best products to show on your shop, how to price your items, and how to really get the attention of your target audience. Without this kind of market research, you are basically working blind in this process and could be hurting your changes of success. Take some time to work with the different aspects of the marketing plan, using both primary and secondary research as well as qualitative and quantitative research so that you get the best picture of your potential customer as possible.

CHAPTER SIX

MARKETING YOUR HOMEMADE PRODUCTS WITH ETSY

It is not enough to just list your products on Etsy and hope to make a good income in the process. There are so many other sellers, hundreds if not more in each category, that without the proper marketing strategy, your product is going to get lost and it will be a miracle if any customer ever finds you. Luckily, there are some great marketing strategies that you can use that will help rank your product higher and make you a good income.

The product

Before you get started with any of the other steps in the marketing plan, you need to make sure that your product is high quality. Yes, Etsy is a homemade site, but that doesn't mean that people aren't expecting high quality. In fact, since most of the products on this site are more expensive than Walmart or other options, the product is often expected to be higher in quality.

So you need to make sure that there is a lot of attention to detail and craftsmanship that goes into all your products. Your customers will be able to tell if the item is well made and if you succeed in impressing them, you will get some great reviews.

Always remember that you need to create a product that is unique. While it is tempting to go for a product that is already on Etsy and doing well, buyers are going to notice when your product is copied and they won't make a purchase. Unique and original products do really well on Etsy so make sure you pick out something you can make and work on that will really show off to the customers and will make them want to make the purchase.

There are so many great products that you are able to produce that will impress the customer, but make sure that you are picking products that are unique and that you actually enjoy making. Customers can tell the difference between products that were just thrown together quickly to make money and those that were given the right time and attention and that the seller really enjoyed putting together. Your reviews are going to reflect how much you enjoy making your craft so always stick with something that you are passionate about.

The photos

Every listing that you put up should have some photos to go with it. This is going to help the customer get an idea about your product so they can determine if it is the right one for them. Etsy has a high standard when it comes to pictures so make sure that you get some good ones. Never use pictures from your phone because these just aren't going to work. Some tips for taking a good picture for Etsy include:

- Take at least a few pictures for every listing. Do different angles of the item as well.

- If the product can be used, show it. For example, if you are selling a hat, show someone wearing the hat.

- Have a background that is plain and doesn't have distractions.

- Have a background that is the same, or at least similar, for all of the products to make it look cohesive.

- Always use a natural source of light to make the product look nice.

Your photos are one of the firs things that your customers are going to see when it comes to your shop on Etsy, or even when you are working on social media. You need to give them the time and attention they deserve so that you can make high quality pictures that will capture the eye and encourage the customer to pick your product rather than going with someone else's product. Take your time, experiment a few times, and even ask for some help from someone who knows how to do photography if you are stuck for ways to make the product pictures better.

Tags

In addition to having a good title for your product, you will get the opportunity to use 13 tags to help describe the item to the buyers and to help the item show up on SEO. You should use all 13 of the keywords and make them count. A good way to utilize the tags correctly is to think just like the customer. What would they put into the search bar when they are looking for your product? You can include color, function, style, occasion, and other names for the product. Make sure that the tags are proper; you do not want to find your product showing up in lists that it doesn't belong.

If you are unsure about how to fill up all 13 slots, try different word combinations. When you mix and match words around, you can come up with a few more. Alternate names and even spellings can help you to catch a few different customers who may not spell the words right. It may seem like a challenge on some of your products to come up with this many names, but it is going to ensure that you are getting as many people as possible so use all 13 each time.

Never underestimate what you are able to do with the tags on your products. This is kind of like the SEO part of your Etsy store. If you do not put any tags on your product, it is going to be almost impossible for the customer to find you or for you to show up in searches on Etsy. You need to use all 13 tags and try to figure out the words and phrases that your customers would use when looking for a product similar to yours. This will make it easier for you to come up at the top of the Etsy searches so that you can make a sale.

Categorizing

At the top of the listing, you will be able to pick three levels of categorizing. You should pick the one that matches the most to your item. You can also choose options for style, occasion, and recipients a swell. Use these only if the item falls into the option perfectly, otherwise you box yourself in a bit.

You may want to be a bit careful about this point. Categorizing can help, but if you have an item that can fit into various categories, it can get you stuck and you won't be able to catch the customers that you want. For example, you may have an item with a sign that says Happy Birthday, but if you allow for customization so that the sign says other things, it is best to not categorize this under birthdays or you will miss out on other customers who may be looking for wedding, anniversary, graduation, and other gifts. But if you are selling a wedding dress, it is fine to categorize your items under wedding.

Customer service

There are going to be many times when the customer will want to ask a question or communicate with you. Many of your items may be customizable and the customer will want to know what changes they are able to make, what the shipping rules are with you, and even to thank you after they order your product. It is important that you keep up with talking to them and providing the best customer service possible, whether they are a new client or have already made a purpose.

Etsy is really easy to communicate on; you just need to make sure that you are available to answer these questions. Ignoring the customer is gong to result in the loss of a sale as many of the customers will comment or message to ask a question about the product or if they are able to customize it. When you are communicating with the customer, make sure to respond to them as quickly as you can, be helpful and polite, and make sure that the customer has a great experience working with you.

Branding

One of the best ways that you can work to make your shop stand out is to do some branding. Branding on an online store can sometimes be a challenge, but often the process you use to package and then ship your goods can help you to brand your business. Some of the ways that you can provide branding on your online store include:

- Provide enough packaging so that all the items you send are going to make it to the customer safely.

- Add a bit of packaging inside the box that is cute. The packaging doesn't have to be complicated, perhaps a ribbon or lace to tie things up, but it does show that you took some extra time on the shipping.

- Add in your business card.

- Find a way to include something extra in with the purchase

- Send a thank you note that was hand written.

In addition to sending out something extra special with your packages, you need to take another look at your store front. You should have a cohesive look present between the shop and the pictures and your shop needs to be as organized as possible.

One issue that some people run into is when they sell a variety of items. If you have clothing and food items in the same shop, it is going to look like a bit of a mess and could make things hard with branding. If this is the case for you, consider opening up another shop and keeping clothing in one and the food items in another.

Things to remember about your listings

The way that you list your items is going to make a big difference on the amount of sales that you make and whether the customer is gong to be able to find your listings. Some of the things that you should remember when it comes to your listings include:

Spread the listings out

If you have a bunch of new items that you are working on, it can be tempting to try and release them all at once. But this can be a bad marketing strategy. Rather, consider releasing them one at a time, usually over a few days. This will help to spread the items out over the search results. Plus, Etsy often places the newly listed items right on the front page so this allows your shop to get some extra exposure right away.

Auto-renew items that sell

If your store is planning on selling and reselling the same items over again, it is a good idea to set the quantity of item pretty high, perhaps at 100. This allows the posting to renew itself after each sale. This helps you to avoid gong out of stock on the site and missing out on some of the clients that you should have.

Make sure to check in on your items as well so that you can see if they are running low and if you need to "put" more back in stock.

Finding buyers

The trickiest part about any business is that you need to go out and find buyers. You could have the nicest shop on Etsy with a great product, but if you do not have the right customers coming in, you will never make a sale. You should consider talking the shop up to your friends and family to perhaps get a few sales, or they can send your information over to some of the people they know.

One thing to keep in mind is to have business cards on hand all of the time. Then when you meet someone new, or run into an old friend, try to find a way to bring up your new business. Talk up what you do and why you love it so much. When you are done, make sure to give them one of your business cards so they can look up your shop later, see some of your selections, and hopefully make a purchase. You may not make a sale each time you talk to someone, but it is the best way to get started with making some connections, sharing the news, and getting people to purchase your product.

Social media

While many people talk about the benefits of using social media all the time, this is not always the best idea. First, with an Etsy shop, you are going to hopefully be busy creating a product all the time and you won't be able to spend hours online trying to keep up with your social media accounts. That being said, Etsy does make it a bit easier to keep up with your social media.

For example, Etsy does allow you to automatically link your Twitter and Facebook accounts to your shop. Other Etsy shoppers can follow or like your shop to keep up to date on new products. You can also start up a page on Facebook that will show the different products or link back to your Etsy page.

One of the best social media sites to use for Etsy is Pinterest. You can create one that is just for your Etsy shop or use your own personal account. This one is a nice site to work with because you can post pictures and descriptions, with direct links that go back to your page for the customer to make a purchase. You can also go on and create a board of things with similar products so that you can bring in more customers.

In addition to using Pinterest to link back to your site and to show off some of the pictures, you may find that using Facebook can be nice as well. This allows you to put all of your customers in one spot (by asking them to join the page) and you can have one place where you put all your updates, information about new products, coupons and discounts for the customers, and other information. It can be a great place to put all of your information so that all the customers are able to find it.

There are quite a few social media accounts that you will be able to choose from and we will discuss a few of them in later chapters. There are a few key things that you will need to keep track of when choosing a social media site. First, make sure that you stick with just a handful of sites. There are quite a few that you can pick from, but if you end up spending more time on social media rather than working on your product, it is going to show in your postings. Pick just a few and devote your time to these.

In addition, make sure that all of your postings are personal. You want to show the customer something important about you. You do not want to annoy them with too many postings, too much sales, and other bothersome tactics. Instead, you want to show a bit about your life, show why you are passionate about your products, and even take the time to share other interesting news that relates to your products.

Blog

It is a good idea to snatch up a domain name early on, one that is gong to go along with the shop name on Etsy. This can be helpful if you decide to start your own website or blog to help promote and sell your products. A blog can be one of the best ways to bring in new customers and keeps your shop high up in the rankings.

You should take the time to write frequent articles to the blog so that you can keep customers coming back. In addition to featuring some of your favorite homemade items in your shop, you can talk about some of the other favorites that you have found on Etsy. Add some coupon codes and giveaways on the shop, talk to other shop owners and have those interviews there, and just work the blog so that it can really appeal to the customers and make them come to your shop instead of someone else's.

If you do not have the time to work on your blog (hopefully this is true because you just have so many orders coming in), consider finding someone who can do the work for you. There are lots of professional writers who can take over the blog writing for you, putting up as many articles as you need each week, to ensure that the blog stays up to date, has the right keywords, and will entice customers to come to your site.

Sales and coupons

Sales and coupons can be a great way to get customers to pick your store over another one. And if you are a seller who does seasonal items or likes to move your inventory around, having a clearance category in your shop, or offering coupons, can be the right option. For those who have social media followers, these clearance and sale items are great things to post on your sites because customers like to get a deal when they buy something.

Etsy makes it easy to create your own coupon codes. You just need to go to the Promote section on your shop and click on "coupon code." You can choose from a variety of options including a fixed discount, a percent discount, or even free shipping. You can even have Etsy send out these coupon codes as a thank you to new customers when they place an order with you. Take the time to put on expiration dates, minimum purchase prices, and more to make the coupon code unique to your store.

A good way to get customers with these codes is to offer them to some of the customers you have had in the past. Send them a new coupon code for being a repeat shopper. They already know how great your products are and may be willing to make a new purchase, with the incentive of your coupon, and you have just made a few new sales.

Word of mouth

If you provide fantastic products and some great customer service, you are going to get new customers easily. Your past customers will not only keep coming back, but they will go and talk to their friends about the amazing products they purchased. Of course, you do not have to wait until your customer's start talking you up, you can do some of the word of mouth advertising as well. Get a few business cards and have them on you all the time. Sometimes you may need to make an opportunity to talk about your products, but try not to be too pushy in the process.

Word of mouth is going to be one of the best ways that you can promote your products and make some sales. Make sure that you are taking care of your customers and that they are really happy with their products. Go to some craft fairs in your area and talk up your product. Go and meet with family and friends and see if they would help to promote your business as well.

People always want to make a purchase from someone they know and trust, or someone they have heard about from another person. Make sure that your name is the one that appears when they are looking for your product, and you can make a ton of sales with your Etsy site.

While many people feel that they should just post a few pictures of their product online and that is enough to help them to bring in some customers, there are thousands of sellers on this site and if you do not put in some of the legwork, you are going to be disappointed in the sales. Creating an effective marketing plan using some of the suggestions listed n this chapter will make it easier for customers to find your products and perhaps make the purchase so that your products start to sell!

CHAPTER SEVEN

HOW TO USE SOCIAL MEDIA TO SELL MORE

You should spend a bit of your time working on social media and reaching out to some of your customers. There are many customers who may not be willing to check back at your store all the time, but they are interested in checking out your Facebook or other social media sites to hear about your products, new deals, and other information. Here are some great tips that you can follow to ensure that you are getting the most out of your social media sites so that you are able to sell more products.

How to use social media
Sell the products, sell yourself

Your customers want to come to your social media sites to learn something. They want to see some of your products, hear some news, and maybe even learn a bit about yourself. You need to sell your products, but also allow the site to show a bit about you and be more personal. Do not use the social media site just as a promotion, let your site tell a bit of a story and allow the customers to come a bit into your own life. Customers are more willing to buy products where they know the story behind the work, where they feel like they know the person who makes the products. Do not be scared to tell your story and see what a difference it will make.

Pick a few sites to work with

It is tempting to want to work on every site that you can find. There are many that you can choose from, and many beginners will choose to go with as many of them as they can so that they do not miss out on any of their potential customers. While this may seem like a good idea, it is actually going to backfire on most people.

There are just too many sites that you can be on and you do not have the time to keep up with all of them. If you sign up for more than a few, you are going to spend too much time working on social media, trying to schedule posts and keep up with questions, that you will alienate customers because you can not keep up with the work and won't give it your all.

So just pick two or three sites that you really like and feel will work for your products. You can devote your time to these, really showcasing your work, and making sure that you create a connection between you and your customers. This is going to get you so much further than you will find with going on too many sites because your customers will be able to tell the difference between you showing your genuine self, and you just trying to make sales.

Get that profile filled out

The profile is one of the most important things on your social media account. This is where the customer is going to look first to see who you are, what you sell, and other information about your business. You need to make sure that you are filling this profile information out completely to help answer questions and to get your customers more interested.

First, start out with a good name; if your business already has a name, you can use that. You will also need to fill out the about me part as much as possible, explaining a bit about who you are, what you sell, and some of your product information. The contact information is important if you want your customers to purchase some of the products that you are selling so include a phone number if you would like or your Etsy shop site for the customers' use.

Make sure to add in some pictures as well. You will need a profile and cover picture to start, perhaps showing you or some of your products. Add in some other pictures to show off the products; you can store these in an album that is saved on the profile so that the customers are able to take a look when they first visit your website.

Experiment

What works for one person is not always going to work for you. But that doesn't mean that you should not give it a try. You may need to try a few different ideas in your campaign before you find the one that is going to work the best for you. Do not be scared to try something that is a bit different and see how well it is going to work for you. You may be surprised at what works for your product that didn't work for someone else.

Make sure that you give each experiment a bit of time. You can not try out something new for two days and then give up assuming that it is not going to work. Give it a few weeks to a few months to see how your customers are reacting. You can always make changes later on if you do not like how something is working on your social media account.

Answer questions as soon as possible

Your social media site is a great place for your customers to come and learn more about your products, but there are going to be times when they will have questions. This is a good way for you to interact more with your customers. If the customer responds to your postings or has a question about the business or a product, you need to make sure that you are answering these right away. This is a great point of contact with the customer and if you check the messages and answer back quickly, you are going to get a better chance at making that final sale.

Of course, you are not going to be able to spend all of your time on social media looking for questions and spending your time answering them. You do need to take the time to work on your products and being on your Etsy site. So how do you handle the problem of keeping up with the questions.

A good idea is to pick two times a day when you will answer the questions. Pick a time in the morning and a time at night when you will get online and see if there are any comments or questions that you need to answer. This allows you to help out customers who may be on the other side of the world from you, but won't take up too much of your free time.

Schedule your posts

Being consistent is key if you want to impress your customers and give them a reason to keep checking out your page. If you aren't consistent with your posts, the customer will get bored and stop checking in. But with the right kind of consistency, you will find that customers will check in often to hear more news and to keep up to date on everything that you are promoting.

Of course, there are times when it is going to be difficult to post on a daily basis. Life comes up, you get busy with creating your products, or something else will come up. The neat thing is that many times, you can schedule your postings. Using tools like hootsuite.com can make it easier to manage these postings. You can go on, link up your different social media accounts, and then list your postings and when you would like them to appear. You can write out postings for the whole week and then hootsuite will take care of posting them for you, freeing up some of your time but allowing customers to still get the information that they need.

Keep things interesting

All of your posts should keep the customers interested in your products. Whether you are posting about the product, posting some great deals, or telling a story of some other kind, you need to make sure that they are interesting. Just listing out facts is not going to get you too far; but telling a story, showing how the customer can use the product, or even adding in something silly and funny will help the customer to feel that connection. And with a good connection, you will be able to get the customer more interested in your products.

Ways that you use social media wrong

Social media is one of the best places to market your creative business. You are less likely to use some of the traditional forms of advertising for your business because it usually doesn't work. Social media allows you to market the products better and keep your customers up to date on new products, sales and so much more.

Social media can be great for selling your products, as long as you go through the process correctly. There are so many mistakes that beginners can make on social media that can ruin their sales and will make it hard to for all that work to pay off. Some of the things that you should avoid when it comes to working on social media include:

Unfinished profiles

If you are going to work on social media, you need to make sure that you completely fill it out and make the page look professional. Any customers that come to your Facebook and other social media sites are there for a purpose. They want to see more about you and your products and be kept up to date about any new products or specials that you are having.

This means that you should take good care of your social media pages. You should make it look professional, fill out all of the information about contact information for the customers, post pictures, and put up plenty of wall posts so that your customers can be kept up to date about anything you are working on.

When you feel stuck about how you should organize your business page on social media, take the time to look at some of the pages of your favorite stores. They do not have to be creative businesses; they can be any kind that you admire or use. Take a look at how they organize their social media sites, take some tips, and put them into your own social media page.

Being on too many pages

There are so many great options that you can choose from when picking social media sites. You can be on Facebook, Twitter, Instagram, Pinterest, and more. Many beginners will decide that they need to be on each of these sites. This can spread you out too thinly, making it difficult to keep up with any of them because you are paying attention to too many of them. If you are spending more time working on social media than you are with working on your product, it is time to cut back.

It is often best to pick two or three sites to concentrate on and ignore the rest. Facebook, Instagram, and Pinterest are really great options for new businesses that sell crafts such as those on Etsy. You can spend a few minutes each day telling your customers about new updates, new deals, and about other information that you think is important to your customers.

Too much self-promotion

Yes, you are supposed to use your social media sites to help promote your business and to tell customers about new products and great deals, but too much self-promotion will get annoying. If you are sending out messages many times a day talking just about your products and you are sounding pushy, you will find that your customers get annoyed and they will start ignoring you and leaving the page.

A bit of self-promotion is a good thing and can help your customers learn more about your products and your company. But do not forget to add in some variety. If you find an article that people may enjoy or something that is going to add value to your customers, add it in. As long as the information will add some value to the customers, it is a great idea to add it into the social media site. In addition, try not to post too much, no matter what the topic is about, so that you do not bother the customers.

Lack of consistency

You need to be consistent with your posting schedule. It is best to post once a day or once every few days so that your customers are able to see new information and will have your company in the front of their minds. Luckily, there are a few tools available that will help you to post each day at the times that you prefer, even if you are too busy to do this all the time. You can set up the posts ahead of time for a week or more and then you can concentrate the rest of your efforts on making great products.

You can set up any schedule that you want with social media, just make sure not to post each hour or forget to post for weeks on end so that you can keep your customers informed and happy.

Not spending the right amount of time

Most beginners feel like they do not need to spend that much time on social media. They figure that a post here or there is enough to help them to sell enough products to their customers. But you would be amazed at how much of a difference a good social media campaign will make in your sales.

You will need to spend some time on your social media accounts, updating pictures, sending out good and consistent posts, and talking to your customers when they have questions. These things do take some time to accomplish. But if you set up a plan and set aside time to get these taken care of, you will love how many new customers you will be able to get with your social media account.

Social media accounts are one of the best ways to interact with your customers and make sales. You will be able to run it like the storefront of your business, but with the added benefit of adding more pictures, helping to answer questions for your customers, and to just interact with them in different ways than you will be able to do with other options. Use it to your advantage and see how well you can increase your sales with relatively little work.

CHAPTER EIGHT

PINTEREST—THE PERFECT SOCIAL MEDIA FOR ETSY

There are many times when you may hear about Etsy and Pinterest together. There is a good reason for this. Many of the sellers on Etsy love to use Pinterest as their main site for promotion and selling their products. Pinterest has the best platform for this kind of thing. It relies mainly on pictures to showcase food, projects, and more and customers are able to find you with simple keyword searches, even if they aren't already following your pins. Once they make a purchase though, they can follow you and your boards and still be kept up on all the information for your store.

Many of those who are looking to expand their reach in social media for their Etsy page will do so with the help of Pinterest because of the ease of setting up an account and how it works to attract in new customers. You will simply need to set up an account and start pinning things to your boards.

Now, as a business owner rather than a customer or just someone using Pinterest, there are a few things that you will have to make different. You will need to use your boards to fill up information about some of your products. Do not be too pushy or into the sales at this point. Pinterest is a good place to post pictures about "that cute hat you got for your daughter" or something similar and then just link back to your website. You can put in a bit more information about the product, but let the picture do most of the talking and your Etsy shop have all the information for you.

But it should not just be about you. Take the time to post on other boards, leaving comments or saving some of the pictures of similar products. The more connections you can make, the easier it is for some others to find you as well. The good news is, once you get a customer to post your information on one of their boards, even if they do for a reason other than making a purchase, you are now being exposed to all of their friends as well.

If you feel like Pinterest may be the best place for you to get started on your social media journey with Etsy, here are the six steps that you should remember to do things right.

Open a business account

While you may not think of yourself as a business when you first get started, you should make sure that you sign up for a business account. This allows you to promote your business name and makes it easier to promote some of your products. Being able to use your business name makes it nice since everything will link together, from your Etsy shop, to your webpage, to Pinterest, and business cards when they all have the same name on them. Plus, the terms and conditions on Pinterest state that you must use a business account if you are offering products for sale.

It is pretty easy to set up your own Pinterest account. Just go and visit business.pinterest.com instead of going to the regular page. You will just need to fill out your information and go through the steps and in just a few minutes, your new business account will be set up and ready to run. You can have this and your personal one if you would like, just be careful not to get the information between the two mixed up.

Try to earn sales

Pinterest is a bit different compared to some of the other sites. While it may feel a bit like a competition, you need to focus more on getting the sale rather than on how many followers you have on your team. Yes, followers can be nice, but if you have

1000 followers and no sales, it really is not doing you much good.

You need to focus more on the quality of the message that you are giving out. High quality messages, good pictures, and connecting with your customers is a much better way to earn those sales. It is much better to have 100 followers and 50 sales than it is to have that original 1000 and only make 40 sales.

Join a community

It is easy as a seller to get pulled in to just doing your own work. You can have many boards on Pinterest and then fill them up with your own products and do nothing else. But this is not really going to help you to get ahead in your new business. You need to join in on a community and become part of the Pinterest world if you want to see success.

Pinterest is a big community. It is a group of people, some who sell similar products and some who do not, who are all looking for the new customers and trying to make some money in the process. These individuals can choose to work on their own, or they can go with the more successful option of working with others to promote their business and their products.

So with this in mind, the first thing that you should remember is to not just pin up your own items on the boards.

You should start up with quite a few of these boards and then fill them up with different information. For example, you could have a board that has some of your favorite products, but then have a few boards that are on related topics and pin things from other business pages.

A good example of this is with baby clothing. You would fill up one or two boards with some of your favorite baby clothing or things that you may be having on sale at the moment. Then you could fill up other boards with mothering information, education, nursery ideas, baby toys, child care, and more. The more boards you have (boards that are complete, not ones that just have one or two items on each), the easier it is for some clients to find you.

Once you have a few boards all set up, you will need to keep going and make some more connections. You can follow others and watch what they are doing. You can go through and re-pin some of the different items that they are posting, talk with them, leave some comments, and just interact in other ways so that your name can get out there in front of the customers.

Use the comments

This one is going to take a bit of your time. You will need to go and look at some of the other boards and get ideas and see what is messaged there. You can choose to re-pin some of these as well, but also write some comments. You should pick out comments that are going to be meaningful to the topic at hand, provide some insight or something new, and ones that are positive. Never use this as a way to bring down the seller, but rather bring up some of your own points and explain them to others.

The comments are not necessarily a place to sell your products. Instead, they should just be like what you post on friends and family posts on Facebook or another page. If you get too salesy, you are going to turn away the customers and can even get blocked. You should simply leave some useful information.

For some people, this can be difficult. They do not want to post information without leaving a link or helping others to find out about them. But indirectly, this is still going to work for you. When customers see your name and the useful information that you are leaving behind, they are going to get curious. They may come and check out your page, look around, and fall in love with some of the products that you are selling. If you answer a question that they have, you may have some customers who contact you directly.

This option may seem like one that is taking a lot of time and not giving a direct benefit to your business, but many customers are tired of all the sales and are more inclined to purchase from those who are there to help them out. Be there as support, offer some suggestions, and keep your boards nice and organized, and your customers will come.

Form a group board and invite others to join

There is a feature on Pinterest where you can create a group board and then invite some others to join. These are really popular and many businesses that create similar products like to work on these in order to create some awareness. You can start one of these group boards and make them relevant to the products that you are selling on Etsy. The board's followers can contribute information and help to increase your reach other customers.

Depending on the type of business that you are working with, you may already have some people you want to work with. For example, if a few of you are working on this new project, you can all bring your own posts together. Some businesses like to come together, such as beauty and diet supplements, and they will share the ideas together to help out the customer and to further their reach. Or you can just open up the board to some others who are in your industry and start to meet and learn about each other in the process.

Get into the habit of pinning

If you are going to use Pinterest, make sure that you keep up on the work. It is not going to do you much good to just post a few boards and then never touch them again. Rather, you are going to get lost in the clutter and all that original work will be for nothing.

With Pinterest, you are going to need to keep up with pinning, working on several images each day, most days of the week. You should also try to pin at various times of the day so that you can reach as many people when they first get on Pinterest as possible. You should also not pin in bursts, do a few pins throughout the day so that you can reach as many of your customers as possible.

Your pins need to be high quality as well. Make sure that they contribute to your community, that they are going to interest your customers, and that there is a point to you pinning them. Being random or picking low quality pictures and more will turn customers away and you won't get any sales or followers at all.

Use Pinterest as a visual medium

Pinterest is a visual medium. This means that you need to take some of those high quality photos and put them to use on Pinterest. Most followers are going to find your products based on the pictures that you are posting. So going with the right light, the best staging, and using a camera are going to be really important if you want to find the customers.

You will need to do things a bit differently on Pinterest though. While many sellers will choose just a white background for their pictures of the products, this is not always the best on Pinterest. Many times, using close-ups, some filters, or lifestyle images are going to be more appealing to your customers and will ensure that they are going to look at the pictures and learn more about your products and Etsy site.

Pinterest is a great social media site to use if you want to find customers easily. While other sites require you to go out and find the customers, when you are on Pinterest, you may be able to reach those customers without having to chase them. Using the steps above, it is easier for your customers to find your pictures, see your boards, and go check out many of the great products that you are trying to post. Remember that quality is more important that quantity with any social media campaign so pick out things that will be of use to your customers and work with that.

CHAPTER NINE

TIPS FOR CREATING GREAT PICTURES TO SELL YOUR PRODUCTS

A bad picture is going to wreak havoc on your business. Pictures of your products are one of the first things that your customers are going to see when they are making their decisions. In fact, the customer will often put in a search query and then will be given a long list of pictures and product names that match up. So you need to have some good pictures in place that showcase some of your best products and really catch the eye so that the customer will pick your product over another one.

Inviting, beautiful, and sharp photos are going to be important to selling some of your products on Etsy. Your pictures need to be really able to show your products, such as the size, the color, and even the texture of the product. This may seem like a tall order for someone who is designing kids clothes rather than a photographer, but with some of these great tips, you will be able to make this into a reality.

Get the right lighting

The right lighting can help your product look amazing. If you place the item in a room that is too dark, it is going to cause too much strain on the customer to try and figure out what is in the picture. On the other hand, if you have a light that is too bright, you will find that the picture looks exposed and ruin the look of your product.

A good thing to experiment with is the lighting. You will need to try with the lights on and off, try different flash points, and add light directly to the product or take it off. You may have to take quite a few pictures in the beginning, but you will soon figure out what works the best for your products and can reuse that over and over again.

You may need to experiment with this one a little bit. The flash on your camera is one place to start, but if you are still having issues with that, you may need to experiment a bit with your lighting in the room. Change up the room that you are using, add in a lamp or other lighting source to help brighten up the object, or even try on a few different backgrounds to see what is going to work the best and what will make the product look the best.

Consider the background

The background of your product can make a difference on how well it sales. You should stay away from backgrounds that are too cluttered or ones that will fade out or hide the product itself. The product should be the main focal point in any picture so if you show that picture to someone else and they notice something in the background before looking at the product, you have the wrong background.

A simple white background, or one that is a solid color that doesn't clash with the product, is the best choice to go with. outside shots while wearing the outfit can add a bit more interest in the picture, but be careful about this as well. You need to make sure that the background is not distracting from the product that you are trying to sell.

Go from different angles

While it is possible to take the picture of your product from straight on, this should not be the only angle that you choose. You want to make sure that you show the product from a variety of directions, showing all the features and more about the product. This helps the customer to know if they are purchasing the right product and can save you a lot of hassle and questions from customers who aren't sure about that product.

Styling the pictures

You do have the option of just setting the product you make down on the table, clicking a picture, and posting it to your Etsy account, but this is going to make things boring. Styling the pictures can add some interest to the picture and even highlight some of the features of your product a bit more.

There are a few things that you can do with the styling. First, you should consider the rule of thirds. The rule of thirds makes it easier to draw a point of interest. Most people are more attracted to a picture that has the subject off to one of the sides, rather than right in the middle. This can be in either direction and the picture can go over the middle point, as long as it is not directly in the middle of the page.

While styling the picture, consider having it in use. For example, if you are selling a hat, you may want to wear the hat or have someone wear the different outfits that you are selling. This is more interesting than just having the hat on a hanger and can draw in some more of the customers that you want.

Consider the camera

If you are going to get serious about selling on Etsy, you may want to invest in a new camera. You need one that is going to be high quality and will really capture the product that you are trying to sell. There are a lot of great options to choose from, so you may need to experiment a bit in order to find the one that is best for you.

For those who may not be able to afford a new camera right from the start, you can still use your regular camera as long as you follow the tips above. Any camera can be used to make great pictures as long as you watch the lighting and make the product look as good as possible. One note to keep in mind is that it usually is not a good idea to use your smartphone to take the picture. These can be fine for showing off things to friends and family or taking simple pictures, but they often do not take the highest quality pictures and can make it hard for people to be able to see the details of your product.

While most beginners will assume that the picture is not that big of a deal. They will just snap a quick picture of the product with their cell phone and call it good. But these pictures are low quality and do not look as good as they could. They may even turn away some of the potential customers because the photo quality is poor and they are not able to see some of the details that are inside. Make sure to take your time and really work on the pictures to wow the customers and get them to make a purchase.

CHAPTER TEN

WORKING ON A BLOG TO PROMOTE YOUR ETSY SHOP

One thing that you should consider is working on a blog to help promote your Etsy shop. This is where your own personal website and your knowledge in SEO will come into play. These are going to help you to get more views to the page so that you can make more sales. You can link the webpage to your Etsy account or offer this as another place that you sell the same products. You need to be consistent with your blogging if you want to succeed, but there are many ways that you can do this that you can even find the process to be fun.

The benefits of having your own website

There are so many benefits to having your own website outside of Etsy. First, not all of your customers are going to be using Etsy. There are many who may not have heard about Etsy or they are looking online through Google or another search engine for something to meet their needs. If you are only available on Etsy, you may miss out on some of your potential clients.

This does not mean that you will use this website to get off Etsy and their awesome platform, it just means that you are going to use this website as a way to lead your customers back to the Etsy shop by providing them with some of the information that you need.

Your website is much better for working with SEO. SEO is basically how you make your website and your information compatible so that it is one of the first search results that come up when a customer is searching for your product. You will need to use certain keywords (Google Keyword Planner is a great place to start to find the best keywords), but when used properly in your web page, they can help direct the customer to your blog articles and with the right link, the blog articles can lead right back to your Etsy page.

You can use this website as another link to your sales page. It can help to catch on to some of those customers who just aren't shopping through Etsy, but who would be really interested in some of the products that you have to sell. Make sure to write great blog posts that have a lot of relevant information and you will be able to see great results by putting your blog to work for you.

How to get started with blogging

Getting started in blogging is pretty easy. You will need to have your website, whether it is a personal website for selling the products or just one that you are using in order to write blog posts. Just make sure that you have one in place that is easy to use, is set up to work with SEO and other tools, and that you are able to upload content to it on a regular basis.

Once you have the website that you would like to use, it is time to get to work with blogging. In the beginning, you should consider adding in some new articles quite often. This helps to fill out the website and the page so it looks like you have quite a bit of knowledge on the topic. No one wants to get onto a page and then see that there are only a few articles and no categories present. This is going to reflect poorly on the writer. It is better to write out a few different topics and to wait to start the website until you are able to get enough articles and information to fill out the blog.

After you have gotten the website up and a good number of blog posts in place, it is time to set up a schedule for the blog posts. You may not have time for a blog post each day, but adding new content at least once or twice a week will ensure that the website stays top of mind in search engines and that your customers and potential customers keep coming back to learn more.

Since you are already running your Etsy business, you may not have time to sit down and write an article each day and upload it. This doesn't take too much time, but it can be a pain to do this each day. A better solution is to choose one day per week that you can devote to your writing. Spend an hour or two on Sunday for example and then just schedule the posting for the time and dates that you would like them to show up. This will ensure that new posting are coming up on a regular basis, but will prevent you having to set aside time to do these each day.

Now you need to focus on presenting good content. It is not going to be a good idea to just post random content or to throw together content that doesn't make sense, looks bad, or has a lot of grammar mistakes. High quality is better than high quantity when it comes to representing your shop on Etsy through the blog.

SEO is another thing that you will want to consider. This is going to help your page to rank high when your potential customers search certain topics so you want to make sure that the keywords are placed in the right locations throughout your blog posts. Do not overdo this because it can backfire. For example, if you write a blog that is only 500 words and 50 of those words contain the same keyword, the search engines are not going to rank you highly.

Usually just a few times in the blog (more if it is a longer blog), will be sufficient to helping you rank high in SEO. You want to make the articles interesting to your customers, make the articles relevant, and to avoid issues with overstuffing and making the articles not sound natural.

A good place to start to determine which keywords you should use is by thinking what your customers would look up when looking for products like yours. You can use tools like Google Keyword Planner to test out a few of these keywords and find out which ones are going to be the best for you. Add them in two or three times for a 500 word or so article, and you are doing pretty good. Once you get a good amount of articles inside the website, you will rank pretty high in SEO.

Outside of the keywords, you do have quite a bit of freedom when it comes to the items that you would like to write about in your blog. You do not have to spend all your time writing about the products that you sell. This gets boring and people won't come to your blog all the time just to read about a list of products. Get original and talk about a lot of different topics.

For example, if you are selling children's and baby clothing, you have a ton of topics that you can write on. You can talk about parenting methods, some of the popular new names of babies that year, new milestones that children are making, some controversial parenting topics, pregnancy, and so much more. Make it original and add in your own voice so that the readers will keep coming back.

At the end of all your articles, make sure to include a short disclaimer of some sort that will link the reader over to your Etsy shop. This makes it easy for the customer to check out your items on their own time without feeling pushed. The blog allows them to go and check out your products if they want to, but they also have the option to just read through the articles without pressure as well.

Writing blog articles can be a simple way to help bring new customers to your site. You get the chance to write about topics that you like and with a little bit of SEO planning, you will be able to bring your customers news and information they are looking for as well as a direct link to your Etsy site.

Hiring someone to help you out

If you are not a writer or you just do not feel that you have the time to write all the articles that you need to keep your blog up and running, it may be a good idea to hire a professional writer to do the work for you. They can take on as many articles as you want a week and many of them can work with you to get the articles posted throughout the week. You can also have them write on any topic that you want.

When hiring a freelance writer, make sure that you are finding someone who has a really personal voice. You do not want your blog to sound like it is stilted or like someone fake wrote it. You want to have some personality within the writing, something that will help the customer to connect with your writing so that they keep coming back for more and even consider purchasing one of your products.

Blogging is not always one of the first things that Etsy sellers will think about when they are getting started on their page, but it can be really important to helping you bring in more customers. You will be able to use this as a great SEO tool, one where you will be able to reach various customers who are looking for your keywords, to help them to find your posts. You can then link back to your Etsy shop and hopefully make more sales with this method. Try out some of the tips above and you will be surprised at how quickly you are able to increase your sales.

CHAPTER ELEVEN

THE DO'S AND DO NOTS FOR SUCCESSFUL ETSY SELLING

As a beginner on Etsy, there are a lot of things to manage. You not only need to manage the orders that are coming in, but you need to keep up with questions that a customer may send to you as well as the marketing plan that you come up with to attract new customers to your store. All of this can seem like a lot of work, but it is all required to ensure that you are going to succeed with your Etsy store. Here we will talk about some of the things that you should do, and some of the things that you should avoid, as a beginner who wants to see success while selling on their Etsy store.

Things that you should do

If you want to gain popularity on your Etsy shop and make some good sales with your handmade products, you should make sure to do some of the following tips including:

- Answer conversations politely and quickly—you should never leave a customer waiting for days or longer to get an answer. While you may not be able to answer everything right away (hard to answer when you are sleeping), try to be as quick as possible when answering back. Also, always act professionally in your communications. You are running a business, so act like it when you are selling.

- Send a thank you—when someone orders from your shop, make sure to send a thank you of some sort. You can send an email thank you or add a handwritten one to your packaging. It's something extra that can make the other person feel important.

- Keep the shop looking nice—think of your online shop just like a normal shop. You want to make sure that it looks nice and is organized. Have different tabs for the various options that you offer rather than just throwing them all up at once. If you are selling different products, such as clothes and food, have separate shops for each type to keep things organized.

- Have high quality pictures—many times your customers will choose your product over another because of how it looks. If your pictures are low quality, you could lose customers. Always have these pictures done as nicely as possible to impress the customers.

- Price the right way—sometimes you may be worried about how much to charge for your items. The best way is to determine how much you need to make for this all to be worthwhile and then add in the amount that it will cost for Etsy fees, packaging, PayPal fees, and so on. Do not worry so much about what others are selling the products for, pick the price that is right for the quality of work you are providing. Customers will notice high quality when they see it and they will pay the extra.

- Take a critical look at the product—is your product really that unique and original? Will it appeal to a lot of people? You need to figure out who will be purchasing the product and then make sure that your marketing is going towards them.

- Offer discounts—buyers love to get discounts and if you are able to offer these to them, they may pick your store over another. A good way to offer discounts to a brand new customer is to give the discount if they purchase two or more products. For example, you can set the price of one at $X and then if they purchase a second one it can be $2X-$10 or something similar.

- Give discounts to repeating customers—there is nothing like being rewarded for being a good customer. It is a good idea to set up discounts that are only available to past customers. Ask them to sign up for an email list and then send these out, only on occasion, to offer them a certain dollar amount of percentage off their next purchase. The past customers have already tried out your products and they may be more than happy to try them out again if they get a good discount.

- Use your social media—while you should not spend all of your time on social media, you should spend more time working on your products and your store, there is still a place for marketing on these sites. Pick a few of the social media sites that are your favorites and devote all of your time to these.

- Be careful with the postage. Find out how much it costs to ship to some of the major areas in the country and post those there. No buyer wants to pay $10 for shipping to find out that it only cost you $3 to get it to them. Weigh the items you want to send and then look it up before charging to the customer.

- Fill out the policies—there is a place on your shop page where you are able to list policies. This can help avoid confusion and will protect you later on. For example, if you have certain rules about returns or shipping procedures, lay them out here so that customers can look at them ahead of time.

- Check your conversations regularly—no you do not want to spend all day at the computer, but your customers want to be able to get ahold of you and if you only check these conversations once a week, you are going to lose out on sales. Check two or three times a day and respond to any new or existing conversations as needed. This is often enough to respond quickly, also dealing with time differences in other parts of the world, but also helps you to not be chained to the computer all the time.

- Add the details to the listings—people want to know more about your product. And if you can give them a story, or a celebration this item would be good for, you may entice them to make a purchase. Talk about the process of making the item, how big it is, what you do to make sure that it is packaged correctly and will get to them safely, and more. Also, take the time to fill out all the tags on an item so customers are more likely to find it.

- Try something new—adding new items to your shop can really help to bring in the customers. Plus, it can give you an edge over others because you have all these items in one spot and are more likely to have something that is unique. If you have been curious about trying to make something new, give it a try and see how it works out for you.

- Take good photos—this is the first point of contact that your customers are going to come across. You need to make sure that your customers are attracted to the pictures so they will even take a look at some of the products that you sell in your store. If the products are low quality, you are going to have some issues with getting people to even look at your store. But if the pictures are great, you may be able to attract some new customers in the door.

- Add something special to your products—you need to add in something that is a bit special to your products. Whether it is an attached gift, a thank you note, or something else, find a way to make your product stand out from all the others.

- Have fun—above all else, remember to have fun with your Etsy store. This is a great way to make some money on the side, some people turn this into a full time income, and to work on a craft that you love. Make sure that you are doing crafts and items that really interest you, rather than ones that you do just because they may be popular.

This will help you to stand out with a higher quality product and can make it easier to make the sale.

- Follow the Etsy rules—you will find that Etsy is a great service to use, but if you start going against their rules, you could run into trouble. Make sure that you read through the guidelines that they set and stick with the few rules that are there and you will find that selling on Etsy is a great option for your business.

- Try a variety of marketing techniques—what works for one company on Etsy is not going to work for everyone. Ever seller is working with a different product or product mix so it is hard to find one thing that is going to work for them all. Try out a few different things and see what works the best for your shop.

Things not to do on Etsy

While Etsy is a great website to place some of your products for sale, there are a few things that you need to be careful not to do if you want to do well including:

- Never say something is a bad idea—how would you feel if you asked a seller a question about changing things, and they said no or told you this was a horrible idea? The same goes for all your buyers. You can find a nice way to go around the issue if it is a problem, but never tell the customer that their ideas are bad.

- Never spam the customer—your customer does not want to receive fifty emails a day from you with updates and general information. This can get annoying and they just won't come back with you. While you can start an email listing if you want (and you should keep this correspondence to a minimum as well), it is best to keep the regular email correspondence to a minimum. One email to let them know you received their order and one to say that you have shipped it should be plenty.

- Social media is not that important—while having social media accounts can be nice, you do not need to have these to get started on your shop. These do take a bit of time to get the hang of so even if you get them right at the beginning, take some time to learn about them.

- Never put up bad photos—some new sellers are so excited to get their items on their shop, that they will take a quick one with a phone and then list it with the item. This can look really bad and can keep the customers away. You want to make the picture stand out in the crowd and really show the customer what they are getting. Take some time to take some great pictures rather than rushing it, and you will find that it is easier to make the sale.

- Do not give up on your bad feedback—unlike the other sites that you can sell on, Etsy allows you to use the kiss and make up feature if someone leaves you a bad review. Sometimes there is a simple misunderstanding about the product, such as someone expecting the package to be at their home and it has only been a few days, and you can discuss this with them and get better feedback. It is much better to talk with your customers and find out why they gave poor reviews and if you can work with them to get a better review for your products.

- Never copy someone else—yes, it is tempting to look at another seller and see how successful they are so you copy their ideas. But other buyers will notice when you are copying and they will not want to purchase from you. Unique and original items always sell the best on Etsy so stick with these and you will see the best results.

- Do not get obsessed over the number of sales—sometimes it is hard to look at another store and see that they have sold tens of thousands of items. You may love getting to that point, but you have to start somewhere. Plus, everyone is selling different products so it is kind of hard to compare yours to someone else. Just work hard on producing a high quality product and you will get the sales that you want.

Creating your own Etsy shop does not have to be a big challenge. It is a great way to work on your own business from home while providing customers with something that is unique and original. And since there are thousands of people who are looking for these unique items for their own homes or for a gift, it is a great place to list your products and make a sale all in one place. While you do need to follow some rules and do a bit of marketing to make sure that the right customers are able to find your products, you will find that this is one of the best ways to reach your customers and make the sale.

CHAPTER TWELVE
THINGS NOT TO SELL ON ETSY

When it comes to setting up your Etsy store, there are a lot of great options that you can choose from. Handmade items are the best, especially ones that are really unique and can not be bought anywhere else. Many customers like to come to Etsy to look for one of a kind gifts, and if you are able to provide this to some of your customers, you can make some great sales.

But there are still some items that you need to be careful about selling. These are items that Etsy is not going to allow sellers to do and if you try to sell them, you are going to get banned from Etsy. With all the other items that you are able to sell, you should just stay away from these prohibited items and stick with some of those that Etsy allows. Some of the items that you need to stay away from on Etsy include:

- Alcohol—any kind of alcoholic beverage, whether you make it yourself or you get it from somewhere else is allowed on Etsy. This may seem a little unfair to those who are making their own beverages like this, but since it is hard to ensure that the person who is ordering is the right legal age to consume and purchase in their country, it is for the protection of Etsy and yourself that you do not sell these kinds of products on your site.

- Firearms and weapons—there are some people who can create really beautiful carvings and other things on firearms. And while this is great, you can not sell these over Etsy. This is because it is hard to figure out who is purchasing them on the other side and it may be easy to sell to someone who is underage or someone who is not allowed to have a firearm or a weapon. You can not do background checks when you are on Etsy. In addition, there are a lot of state, local, and country guidelines that have to be followed when selling a firearm and it is not likely that you have the permissions to do so.

- Drugs and any drug substances or paraphernalia. Most drugs are illegal so do not try to send them through the mail after making a profit on them. Even if you make some of the paraphernalia on your own at home, these are not allowed on the site.

- Hazardous materials, such as ones that are explosive, poisonous, and corrosive. You can go down to your local post office and get a list of all the items that are not allowed under this section. If you are not allowed to send it because of the post office guidelines, do not try to sell it on Etsy.

- Live animals as well as any illegal products for animals. You may want to take a look at the products that are considered illegal when it comes to animal products. There are often a few that may surprise you and it can depend on the area you are living. Also, do not send off any live animals. You did not create these so they are not allowed on this crafting sites.

- Real estate—this is not Zillow or another home or real estate selling site. You are supposed to concentrate on selling handmade crafts and most of your customers have no interest in finding real estate anyway so your market is limited. In addition, if you are looking for products on Etsy, make sure that you do not trust anyone who is selling real estate. It is most likely a fake and you are just going to lose money rather than getting the products that you are promised.

- Recalled items—if an item that you have to sell has been recalled, you should not sell it. This is common with many car seats or other children's products. You may need to check into the recalled list frequently to see when new things are added. If you have an item that has been recalled or your product contains an item that has been recalled, you need to avoid selling these right away.

- Pornography—this is a family friend site, do not sell pornography.

- Motor vehicles—remember, this is supposed to be a craft store. It does not make sense to sell motor vehicles of any kind since these are not homemade and craft products. If you have a hat or some clothing to make, you can use Etsy. If you are wanting to sell something like a motor vehicle, check out a local car listing site and see what you can find.

- Human body parts or remains –anything that has to do with the human body should not be sold. Anything that you can think of is to be avoided as this can be completely unsanitary and can make others sick along the way. Pick out products that you can actually make and won't make others sick and you are off to a good start.

- Tobacco and smoking products of any kind—again, this is just like with the alcohol and the firearms, you can not guarantee who is purchasing the item. There are age restrictions, licensing issues, and even rules that govern sending these products over state and country lines and it can cause a lot of issues. Even if you create some of the tobacco products yourself, you will not be able to sell these on Etsy.

- Any item that will promote hatred to other people or cause them to feel demeaned based on their sexual orientation, disability, gender, ethnicity, or race. Remember that there are all sorts of people who use these sites. People from all over the world use Etsy to sell and to purchase items. How would you feel if someone else had items that were discriminating against you and your religions? For this reason, and because you just should not do this anyway, Etsy is not going to allow these kind of products on their website.

- Any item that promotes or otherwise glorifies harmful acts. Harmful acts should not be encouraged when you are working on Etsy. Remember that this is a family friendly business site, so stick with items that adults, children, and people of all ages will be fine with seeing.

- Any item that in any way glorifies illegal activity. This should be common sense so do not go and try to promote any products that glorify or tell others to participate in illegal activities. You should be careful if you are working on things like banners or clothing so that the sayings on these items aren't going to promote one of these things.

If you are getting started on your new Etsy account, you need to be careful about selling any of these items. These items are going to get you banned on the site and could make it hard for you to sell in the future. Stick with simple homemade items, such as shirts, hats, and more, and you will see a lot of success working with Etsy.

CONCLUSION

Working on Etsy can be one of the best experiences that you can do for your at home business. If you create something that is unique or something that you make by hand, you are sure to find a lot of great customers. Of course, you won't be able to just post a picture and hope it all works out; you have to put a little more work behind it and come up with a good marketing plan in order to alert customers of your product and to make the sales that you want.

This guidebook has spent some time talking about how to use Etsy and make it your very own. Anyone can find success with Etsy as long as they learn which options to use and how to make their products more visible to the general public. The good news is that if someone is looking for unique presents or something that is handmade, they will often head to Etsy first so if you can make your shop attractive and ensure that the customers will find you, it is easier than ever to make the sale.

We hope that with this guidebook you are able to get your shop set up, the products listed, and the customers coming in so you can start working and making a great income with Etsy!

Made in the USA
Lexington, KY
15 December 2016